Make Youtube Work For You

Make YouTube Work For You

A Simple Guide for YouTube Success

Contents

CHAPTER 1
INTRODUCTION

The world is evolving; some people share this opinion. The world has fully evolved; yet some other people also share this belief. Either ways, these two statements could be said to be valid depending on the perspectives of the persons arguing. The world has over the years successfully moved on. There is nothing as constant in life as change. Man is a unique animal. His environment keeps changing likewise. However, man's ability then to adapt to the ever evolving environment makes him both unique and special. This is proven as man is the only animal capable of comfortably adapting to the ever changing environment around him.

The world has witnessed series of technological strides from the analogue era to the digital era. How things were viewed 20 years ago is not the way they are now. A Bentley which might have been the toast vehicle of those days will most certainly not meet up with the vehicles been manufactured now. Owning and watching the television set some years back was a luxury only a few rich folks could afford, the television set is not even in vogue anymore. Years back, advertising was optimized using the local media which included the television, radio, billboards, and even newspapers. In as much as all these are still available now, they seem to have worn out their relevance as proper marketing tools as people seem to have moved on from them. So, how then does one reach out to other people now? That is the million dollar question. The saving grace however, is that the answer is not far off. To be able to reach out to many people at the same time, it is only logical to seek out avenues through which you speak to them all at the same time. As we rightly pointed out earlier, we live in a digital age now. The internet has made the world a closely knitted global village where people reach out to others in other parts of the world in a matter of seconds. Almost everyone owns either an internet accessible mobile device or a computer, a great percentage own the two. That been established, one could say then that the internet seem to be a good way of advertising or marketing products to others. This is not entirely false. The internet is the gateway to the world after all. The problem now lies on how to effectively utilize the internet to this effect. We do not have to look any further. Have you ever heard of YouTube? It seems we might have just struck gold. It takes one to have been living in a cave for the past few years to not have heard of YouTube -pardon my sarcasm. YouTube has all the answers we seek. It is the perfect tool for effectively reaching out to the hundreds of millions of Internet users scattered all over the globe in a matter of seconds. One may be tempted to ask some funny questions such as; what is this YouTube all about, how is it used to reach the hundreds of millions of people all over the world at the same time? And a host of other related questions. You need not worry; you are in the right place as all these questions will be answered in the subsequent chapters and doubts, cleared. YouTube is simply the video sharing site that is owned by Google. It is basically a website that allows anyone or everyone to post videos online so that anyone else can also access the website and watch. It is one of the most popular sites around and always fun to be in. Its popularity is shown in its constant ranking in the top five of all the sites on the web with an average 130 million visitors per month. This massive visitor size of YouTube and the almost zero charge of entry make YouTube attractive to the potential entrant. With just a camcorder or even a phone and a computer, the entrant is set for business. Given that a huge number of individuals and companies alike embrace YouTube videos, it should not be surprising then that a variety of ways through which the site can be optimized abound. This is because anything that can be said to a person or a group of persons can just be said in a video and distributed via YouTube. The book aims at dissecting YouTube to the barest in such a way that a beginner, who has no prior knowledge of YouTube can after reading, master the arts and go from just the initial account creation stage to getting paid ultimately. It is a suitable guide for potential successful YouTubers. That been said, it is time to fasten your seatbelts as we take the fun ride to YouTubesville.

CHAPTER 2
OVERVIEW OF YOUTUBE

Launched in May 2005, YouTube allows billions of people to discover, watch and share originally created content in form of videos. It provides a forum for people to connect, inform and inspire others across the globe and act as a distribution channel for original content creators and advertisers- big and small alike. It is interesting that YouTube has more than 1 billion users. Everyday people watch hundreds of millions of hours on the site and generate billions of views. About 600 hours of video are uploaded therein every minute. YouTube is localized in 75 countries and available in 61 languages. About half of YouTube views are on mobile devices. Research has shown that more than a million advertisers are using Google Ad platforms, the majority of which are small businesses.

YouTube was the idea of three friends: Steven Chen, Chad Hurley, and Jawed Karim. The three friends were former colleagues at PayPal who had just left their former employer in search of a new business opportunity. Their original idea about YouTube was to be an online video dating site. They had promised $500 to any lady who successfully uploads videos to that effect in the site. However, their inability to constantly pay the video upload creators changed the course and direction of the site. They eventually realized that there was a great need for a service that supports the process of uploading original content, watching, and sharing videos. This they realized after taking digital photos and capturing videos at a party and being unable to share to each other via e-mail due to differences in file formats and codec. Acting on their inspiration, the three friends set out to achieve their dream, hence YouTube was conceived.

The domain name Youtube.com was officially registered on February 15, 2005 even before the three friends started developing the technology for the site. It is laughable that the initial location for YouTube's development was in Chad Hurley's garage. The three friends infused three types of energy in the development stages, Steven Chen who was considered the programmer worked with Adobe's Flash development language to stream video clips inside a web browser. Chad Hurley who was the user interface expert, adopted the usage of 'tags' which allowed users to easily identify and share any of the videos they liked. Working as a team, they were able to come up with an easy way that enabled users paste video clips onto their own web pages. This expanded the reach of the site. As the development of the site was completed, it became imperative for the site to be tested by the public to ascertain its efficiency. To this effect, a public beta test version of the website went live in May of the same 2005, just three months after the domain name was registered.

The three men were tasked with constantly debugging the site in the early months of its development. They finally decided it was ready for its purpose and officially launched YouTube in December 2005. All the efforts put in by the three men seemed to be rewarded from their first day at work as YouTube proved immensely popular from day 1. It was able to generate a whopping three million visitors in its first month. Some existing professional sites were struggling to get a couple thousand visitors monthly at the time but YouTube even as a start-up generated three million; it was such a great feat. By February 2006, its third month in business, the number of visitors to YouTube had tripled to a nine million visitors. By its seventh month in business (July), it already had thirty million visitors. It eventually attracted well over 38 million visitors by the end of its first year in business. This gigantic figure it amassed in its first year placed YouTube as one of the top 10 sites on the web and ultimately as one of the fastest growing websites in history.

YouTube's achievement in a space of one year was enough to send jitters down the spines of other competing websites. This prompted the biggest of the competing websites setting out to acquire it. It should be noted that YouTube was soaring with the traffic but was not actually booming in terms of revenue as it was still a start-up so this enabled Google which was a big player in the Web industry to buy it off in the October of 2006- barely a year and a few months into its operation. Google paid a whopping $1.65 billion for YouTube. This remains to this day, one of the highest ever payments for a start-up company that had yet to generate significant revenues. The acquisition by Google placed YouTube at the centre of the almighty Google Empire although it still operates independently of Google. Also, the site continues to act pretty much the same as it did in the pre-Google days with volume being the only significant difference.

Today, the number of videos and users on the site continues to grow as it appears YouTube is replacing the traditional television. This is a fascinating trend as businesses are taking advantage of YouTube to reach a larger potential customer base. The market research firm ***comScore*** as at 2010 placed YouTube as the number three site on the Web, attracting 146 million viewers per month. These visitors watch a lot of video contents- even more than two billion videos a day. Google says that an average YouTube viewer spends 164 minutes online everyday whereas viewers also spend only 130 minutes per day watching the traditional television. So would you rather place your advertisements on the traditional television or on YouTube which is better been watched? Your answer is as good as mine. It is surely YouTube without any doubts.

CHAPTER 3

GETTING STARTED ON YOUTUBE: CREATING AN ACCOUNT

Creating an account with YouTube is as simple as it is effortless. The only required components are an internet accessible mobile device or a computer and then an internet connection. Did we mention that creating a YouTube account is free? It is! No charges whatsoever. Only little basic information is required for the username and password to be created. There is no need for personal information such as your phone number, street number or even credit card details. YouTube extracts this basic information from the database of Google for entrants who already have a Google account and they just go straight to creating a username and password at the YouTube site. However, individuals who do not have a Google account prior can easily create a YouTube account by following the detailed steps below;

- From your local browser, access www.Youtube.com and click the **Sign Up link**. The Sign Up link is boldly located at the top-right side of the YouTube default homepage. The link should take the user to the **Create Your YouTube Account** Page.

- You will be required to enter your e-mail address and a password. The only way you scale past this stage is if you provide a valid e-mail address.
- You will then still be required to re-type the Password and Username in the fields. YouTube wants to make sure you are conscious of the password and Username you are using.
- The next is the location drop-down list, where you are required to select the country where you live, not necessarily your country of origin. Citizens of the United States, United Kingdom, and Canada are also required to enter their postal code in the appropriate area.
- The entrant is then required to select his/her gender and enter the date of birth. It is worthy to note that YouTube does not permit persons under the age of 13 to create an account in the site.

- Next up is where you type the characters (in form of letters and numbers) from the visibly coloured box into the word verification field. When the characters cannot be seen or read, the **New Image** link next to the box should be clicked to enable one view a different image and colour scheme.
- You then either check or uncheck the box **Let Others Find My Channel on YouTube if they have my e-mail address**. You either check or uncheck depending on your individual preference. The options tend to give one some control over who sees or does not see your videos.
- Then you check the **Terms of Use and Privacy Policy box** after reading all that is there to be read and accepting all.
- The last step is to click the **Create my Account button**. However, the account will not be created if any field is left empty or when you choose an already existing Username. A refreshed page with red warning notes identifying the fields that

require corrections will always pop up in this case. In the absence of any further correction, the new Gmail account is created. The Gmail account ultimately grants access to YouTube.

CONFIRMING YOUR E-MAIL ADDRESS

YouTube wants to ascertain that the e-mail address you entered during registration is actually valid and active. This is for easy identification and reaching should any issue arise with your account. They want to contact you easily. To achieve this, after the Sign up procedure has been completed, YouTube sends a mail- **YouTube Service** to your account. The mail usually shows up instantly after signing up, but it may take a few seconds to minutes depending on the internet connectivity strength. The mail comes as a sort of welcome note and offers a few highlight of the experience in YouTube. It also informs you of the need it is to confirm your e-mail address through the link sent in the mail. You must first confirm your e-mail address to be able to upload a video or to comment on a video.

The detailed steps in E-mail confirmation include;

- The blue Upload text link in the mail is clicked. When the link is clicked, it automatically takes you to the YouTube email confirmation page

- You enter your email address in the **Send a Confirmation Email to** field
- Click on the **Send Email**
- Visit your email inbox. There should be an email from YouTube titled **YouTube Email Confirmation**. Open the mail.
- Finally, Click on the blue **Click Here text link**. This link takes you to the upload page of YouTube. You may wish to upload a video now or do so at a later time. At this juncture, your email is confirmed making you a full-fledged member. Fully registered members enjoy access to all the features available in YouTube whereas non-members can only watch videos.

LOGGING IN

When an account is registered with YouTube from a particular computer, the computer remembers the username and password and automatically logs you in the next time. However, if you are logging in with a different device or computer, you will be required to enter your username and password. The process is always as simple as ABC. The **Log In** text link at the top-right corner of the page should be clicked. Then your **Username and Password** should be provided in the columns for them. Then you should click on the **Log In** button.

Upon registration with YouTube, one is advised to write down his username/ password and keep carefully especially if they are different from the ones used regularly on other sites. However, in the event of one forgetting his username or password, you just have to follow the simple steps given below;

- Click the **Log In text link** at the top-right corner of the page.
- Click the Password text link next to **Forgot** below the Log In button. This takes you to the Forgot Password page. If you want to retrieve a forgotten username rather, click the **User Name text link** instead.
- Enter your username. This shows you are the original owner of the account.
- The verification code from the multi-coloured box should be entered in the required field.
- Click the **Email my Password** button.

If the above steps are followed systematically, YouTube will send an e-mail containing your password to your registered e-mail address.

CHAPTER 4

BUILDING YOUR YOUTUBE CHANNEL

Just as colleagues in the same company have their separate and unique offices or cubicles at the least, all users of YouTube also have their personal space in the site. This personal space is known as a channel.The channel is like your home on YouTube. It is somewhat a fancy name for what should be ordinarily known as a profile page. This channel can be said to be a broadcast page where all the uploaded videos of a user appear. Channel creation is the sole responsibility of YouTube. Every user is automatically assigned a channel once the first video is posted. When your house is not in order, there is no way it would attract people. Other users who wish to see all the videos you have uploaded on the site do so by accessing your channel. Users who also want to be notified by YouTube whenever you upload a new video can subscribe to your channel. The relevance of channel in YouTube can never be overemphasized as it is one of the make or mar factors. The channel URL is the link that one shares to the public to direct them to his channel page straight up. It is very important then, that one takes time to build this channel to such a taste that will surely delight other users who visit. YouTube users access your channel to see more of you and probably connect to your business so it should be worth it for them.

Characteristics of a YouTube channel

All YouTube channels have certain things in common. They include;

- The user information, it also includes a link to subscribe to this channel.
- All the videos uploaded by the owner of the channel.
- The favourite videos of the user.
- All the comments on the user's channel.
- Links to connect to the user, via comments, e-mails, and the likes. It may also contain a link to the owner's non-YouTube website.
- Links to the user's groups, playlists, friends and the likes.

- All the channels the user is watching.

It is safe to say then that your channel is your personality on YouTube and should be treated with great caution and care. When a viewer likes what he sees on your channel, he can then subscribe. The viewer upon subscription gets notified by email whenever the channel user uploads any new content on YouTube. All a viewer has to do to subscribe to a channel is simply to click on the **Subscribe button** on the channel page.

SELECTING A NICHE ON YOUTUBE

When a footballer is fouled in the penalty area of the football pitch, he is most times awarded a penalty kick. When he steps up to take the kick, his mind is already made up on which side of the goalpost he is directing his shot at. He then goes on to take the kick. We are not concerned with the outcome of the kick in this book. What we take from the illustration is that the footballer makes up his mind before taking the kick. He doesn't do the thinking as he is taking the kick. In the same vein, anyone who intends to start a successful YouTube channel should as a matter of importance decide on what niche to target. We can define niche in this context as the substance that make channels stand out. It is like a subject or topic that the videos in a particular channel are centred on. We already established that the channel is a homepage. You do not want to be a jack of all trades and master of none, it is always advisable to focus on a particular niche and direct all the energy in it. Examples of niches include tutorials, Vlogs, food, fashion, gaming and the likes. Selecting a niche beforehand allows one to know the audience he is targeting and to know the best strategies to apply for the actualization of the plan. A retired footballer who is setting up a YouTube channel may wish to select the football analysis niche as he would probably still have an undaunted passion for the game. A make-up artist may wish to select the fashion niche as that is his area of specialty. For the sake of the starter who might not have any particular niche in mind. I will be listing and explaining some criteria to be considered before choosing any niche. They include;

- Passion
- Demand
- Competition

PASSION

This is where you ask yourself very sincere questions and answer them honestly. The user should ask the self whether the topic he is considering choosing genuinely fascinates him. Is this something you can regularly make passionate videos about? The money you seek to make in YouTube may not start flooding in from day one. It might take a while before the pay day sets in. Constant uploading of interesting content is also vital to keep the viewers glued to the channel and to even reach out to other viewers. Will you be passionate enough to constantly make and upload videos even without the money coming in? When you are not passionate about the niche then, it becomes a problem. This is because a time may come when you run out of ideas and frustration sets in. When one is passionate about a particular thing, he will always tend to get fresh ideas from just about anything. When one is not passionate about a subject on the other hand, he is likely to get bored easily. When you listen to someone who has real passion for something speak, you are drawn even more into what he is saying. Therefore, passion is vital in niche selection.

DEMAND

Demand and supply are the basics of any business venture. When you go about supplying what people do not want, what do you think happens? You end up being your only customer. The same applies in YouTube. In niche selection, you have to research and know for certain if there are demands for the subject you which to explore. This is particularly important when you hope to make money on YouTube. When people do not watch the videos you upload, there is nothing for you. Therefore, a deep research should be embarked on to ascertain the topics that most of the audience watch often and consider pitching a tent therein. The Google Ad words Keyword Planner can be employed to check the number of searches per month on certain search queries. The Google Trends is also an important tool that shows the different popular topics over time.

COMPETITION

One of the greatest challenges that new entrants in the YouTube world face is getting acknowledged. This is as there are obviously already good YouTubers in the stage prior to their arrival. It is a very competitive game that requires hard work, steadfastness and patience. It is always good to go for niches that are not oversaturated as competition will be less there. It is also advised to go for niches with high demand and low competition. But then, fortune favours the brave right? If your mind is already made up on a particular niche you feel you can make an impact on and it seems highly competitive, brace up and face the battle head-on. Targeting keywords with low competition and simultaneously working your way up the ladder might be all you need as well. Your contents should always improve on what other Youtubers in that niche are doing. You have to analyse what others offer and their limitations. This can be gotten from their comment sections where viewers may suggest for certain things. Then do your best to incorporate everything in the contents you are delivering. You can as well look for ways of presenting situations from other angles. There is no one way of doing things. It is a competition after all. Adding that extra value to the viewers should be the watch word in everything you do. To win in a competition, you have to stand out from the crowd. To stand out from other Youtubers, you should be offering what they do not even dream of offering yet. Competition requires one to be unique in thinking and approach.

CHOOSING A CHANNEL NAME

This is the first step in creating or building your YouTube channel. The name is likely to live with the channel forever so proper care should be taken to ensure that that this name aligns with your brand. The name should be able to clearly communicate the concepts in your channel. There should also be a relationship with the name and your other social media channels. To rename the channel name on YouTube, the following guides should be able to walk you through;

- Go to YouTube and sign in with your Google account
- Go to **settings** (the wheel-like icon found in the menu at the top right)

Religiously follow the steps there to either **create** (if you have not yet uploaded any videos) or **rename** your channel (if you have already uploaded videos) and see your channel ID.

CUSTOM ICONS AND PROFILE PICTURES

For your channel page to look even more attractive to your viewers, some icons therein have to be personalized and given a better look. To do this, the down arrow next to the username at the top of any YouTube page is clicked. **My Channel** is then selected. Your current channel page is displayed with a host of buttons for editing aligned along the top. These buttons include: **Settings**, **Modules**, **Themes and Colours**, and **Videos and Playlists**. Each of the buttons are then clicked to edit as deemed fit by the user.

TO EDIT CHANNEL SETTINGS

When the **settings tab** is clicked on, a new settings panel that lets you edit your channel's page title as well as other features pop up at the top of your channel page. The settings you can edit in YouTube are; the **channel page title**, the **channel type, channel tags** (keywords), **Make Channel Visible (yes/ no), let others find My Channel on YouTube if they have My Email Address (Yes/ No**). The appropriate changes are made and the **Save Changes** button clicked when done.

TO EDIT CHANNEL THEMES AND COLORS

The channel page's look and feel is determined by its themes and colours. When the **Themes and Colours** tab is clicked, it expands the top of the channel page and displays the themes and colours pane. Any desired colour or theme is then clicked on to switch the channel to that theme. For even more personalization, the **Show Advanced Options link** is clicked on to expand the themes and colours pane further. This link has options to control the colour of various page elements. It also enables you to even add your personal background image to the channel page. This is a very good way of displaying your business or product logo. To display the background image, you just have to click on the **Choose File button** in the background Image section and select a JPG format image for the background. The image can be displayed once on your page (in the case of default), or repeated through a longer page (in the case of the repeat background option). After applying the necessary changes, the **Save Changes** button is clicked on.

TO EDIT THE CHANNEL MODULES

The channel module is edited so as to control what contents can be displayed on the channel page. Content modules such as **Comments, Friends, Groups**, Other **Channels, Moderator, Subscribers, Recent Activity**, and **Subscriptions** can be displayed or not depending entirely on what the user wants. You just have to click on the **Modules** tab to display the modules pane and the necessary adjustments are then made. As with others, the **Save Changes** button is clicked on when done.

TO EDIT VIDEOS AND PLAYLIST

This is where you customize the videos that are displayed on your channel page. It grants you access to choose which video you want displayed in the **Featured video** of the channel. When the **Videos and Playlists** tab is clicked on, you may now choose to display **My Uploaded Videos**, **My Favourites**, or **Playlists**. You may also choose between the default Player view and a grid view. You can as well decide to automatically play your featured video when your channel page is opened. When the necessary changes have been made, click the **Save Changes** button.

CHANNEL DESCRIPTION BOX

It is safe to say that the YouTube description box is the most undervalued player in the channel. This is so because many Vloggers, YouTube marketing teams and business channels often regard the description as irrelevant. How wrong they are. They do not seem to realize that the description box is a crucial player because its content helps YouTube in determining where videos rank on search. The description box gives the viewers a short overview of everything they should expect from your channel. It should not be joked with. It is ideal that the description should be written before the first video is made public although it can always be edited. The first five lines of the description box are very essential. This is because the first two lines are displayed next to your video when the video is posted to the social media or in search. Also, the first five lines are included beneath your uploaded video above the **Read More** tab. It is advised to always include a link to your personal website in the first two lines. The description box allows up to 1000 characters, they should all be used. Writing catchy 100-200 words in addition to the first 5 lines shows Google that you have a meaty content. Keywords are very essential and should be used in the description box.

CHAPTER 5

INTRODUCTION TO YOUTUBE STUDIO

The YouTube Studio or YouTube creator studio can be said to be a branded toolset which is built into YouTube that allows users to manage their accounts better, better interact with the teeming viewers, and organize the video content generally. The YouTube Studio comes with a lot of beneficial tools some of which include the analytics and community tabs. These tools ensure YouTube users get more leverage from their channels. The analytics helps in keeping track of certain video metrics whereas the community tabs monitor the comments on uploaded videos. A mastery of the YouTube studio gives one an edge because the analytics it provides ensures you have better content to dish out to the audience. The YouTube studio has many elements and they include;

- YouTube studio dashboard
- YouTube studio analytics
- YouTube Studio manager
- YouTube studio community
- YouTube studio channel
- YouTube studio audio

The YouTube Studio dashboard is of great importance to your potential video marketing. This is as some of the tools it comes with show your most important metrics at a glance. This serves as a good room for comparison where you see how your videos are measuring with others. The dashboard also shows the user certain metrics that help in analysing recent subscribers. It generally aids the user in gaining even better insight into the industry.

The YouTube studio analytics is where the magic happens. It shows the user in clear terms the videos which are working and which are flopping. It is so beneficial to the user because with the information gotten here, you can then go ahead to create videos that will attract your audience because you already have a pre-information.

The YouTube studio video manager is a reliable and easy way to edit certain details of videos to make them appealing to the audience. You may choose to change the description, to edit the thumbnail, and even change the title to ensure that the videos look enticing to the target audience.

The YouTube Studio community helps in engaging viewers interactively through comments. Responding to comments is a very effective tool in marketing- no matter how negative the comment seems. The YouTube Comment tab helps in replying to comments.

The YouTube Studio channel aids the user to be abreast with the channel's information. The information goes a long way in letting you know your channel's abilities.

The YouTube Studio audio allows the user to select music and sound effects that align perfectly with his video. The interesting part is that it is entirely for free! Now if that is not awesome, I do not know what else could ever be.

CHAPTER 6
CREATING VIDEOS

We can say that YouTube is video, and video is YouTube. It is all about the video. You must have seen your share of bad videos in the past. Do you still remember how angry it made you feel? I am sure you still do. For the sake of anything you hold holy, please do not make others go through the same stress and anger when they click to watch your own videos. Anyone who is ready to grow and subsequently sustain a loyal subscription base on YouTube has to start by laying a very strong creative foundation. The user with the intent of creating a video should take it upon him to answer some honest questions based on conditions. He has to ask himself if the viewers can share the videos without having second thoughts or doubts, You have to ask yourself whether making the video felt like talking to a real audience because videos are meant to be conversational, You have to ask yourself if the audience can interact with the content. Consistency is key if you want to stick around and make that money, you ask yourself if there are consistent elements leading up to the next episode, You should make videos with your target audience in mind, if you were to be your own audience, how will watching your video make you feel? You should also have to consider whether your video will be discoverable through search, Above all, you cannot sell it by faking it, are your videos actually a depiction of true passion? When they are stemmed from passion, it tends to inspire. For a particular video to be successful, it must solve the problem it set out initially to solve.

There are some tips on how to make even more effective videos. They are;

- Always shoot for the smaller screen
- Balance the contrast
- Keep it slow and steady
- Invest in quality equipment
- Shoot like a pro
- Use two cameras
- Look professional – or not
- Consider creating a slideshow

- Hire a pro
- Break the rules
- Be entertaining
- Be informative
- Go for the funny
- Keep it short
- Keep it simple
- Stay focused
- Communicate a clear message
- Connect through emotion
- Appeal to viewers values
- Be interactive

SHOOT FOR THE SMALLER SCREEN

Most of YouTube viewers access the site with their small windows computers or even mobile devices these days. The content creator should take this into consideration whilst creating the video. Watching videos meant for big screens on a small screen is such a torment for the viewer. Certain details get lost. The best videos in YouTube are usually the ones that exploit its standard display. It is advised to leave the frivolities off. No fancy background, no unwanted details, just the speaker's face big in the frame. The best YouTube videos are visually simple. It is advised you get up close with the camera and frame the subject so that it fills most of the screen. You should zoom into the main subject when using a camcorder, removing all the irrelevant people or objects from the frame. In summarily, close-up shots are good whereas crowd shots are not.

There should also be adequate lighting in the set that you are shooting your scene. Some YouTube videos have been criticized of being too dark; you do not want your own to join the already existing list. Some web-cam companies would always claim their products work efficiently under normal room light; a set of photo floodlights will work even more efficiently. Get the affordable ones!

BALANCE THE CONTRAST

Visual contrast is highly necessary with videos. Putting a pale or white subject in front of a black background balances the colour equation. Also, putting a black-clad subject in front of a black one does the tricks as well. The colours should always be balanced. It is advised to always make use of brightly coloured backgrounds. YouTube thumbnails usually select images with brightly coloured backgrounds. Hot pink colour has a way of grabbing the attention of casual viewers. It is left for you to optimize colours to your own advantage and turn those casual viewers into subscribers. However, too much contrast can be detrimental. Webcams and camcorders interfere with too much colour. The only way to check the right balance of contrast is by testing your shooting environment before going ahead with the video.

KEEP IT SLOW AND STEADY

While shooting videos, it is imperative to master the craft well. There is no need to rush into aspects you are not yet familiar with. Moving the camera too fast or having the subject move too fast may result in the viewer seeing motion smears and some other video effects. Things should be kept slow and steady for optimal results.

INVEST IN QUALITY EQUIPMENT

For a good and quality video to be made, a good and quality video camera is required. The quality camera should not necessarily be a professional camera. A quality video can be achieved with the aid of a high-quality consumer-grade camcorder. A digital camcorder is always preferred to an analogue equivalent. The world has gone digital after all. The digital camcorder records the video entirely in the digital format. Some qualities to be looked out before getting a camcorder are; Ones that work well under low-light conditions, quality lens with nice zoom factor, compactable with an external microphone. Hard disk camcorders make it easy to transfer video from camcorder to the computer for editing and should be sought. The preferred camera's charge-coupled device (CCD) size has to be big for a better picture quality. You should also consider investing in high video editing software likewise. If your computer specification is not fascinating enough, getting a better one is not entirely out of place.

SHOOTING LIKE A PRO

We know you are not a professional yet. That notwithstanding, you should always apply the best measures to ensure you come out with the best possible video. The only way to achieve this is by embracing the professional production techniques. These measures should be religiously adhered to;

- Manually set the focus on your subject when recording a night scene. Some camcorders that are automatically set tend to focus on the brightest subject in a scene. The subject in this case may not be the brightest piece resulting in the camcorder focusing on an irrelevant whack.
- Use an external microphone often. You should not rely on the sound prowess of the camcorder; it can never be as good as an external microphone. The mechanical noise from the camcorder motors will always distort the sound production. Use an external microphone whenever possible.

- Do not move the camera around too much
- The camera should be kept steady. This can be achieved by using a tripod.
- Do not use digital zoom. When the digital zoom of the camcorder is used, it uses the highest available optical zoom which crops the image to a smaller part of the scene. What this means is that in a bid to zoom objects, the camcorder ends up redrawing pixels which certainly results in poor quality.
- The background and crowd noise should be eliminated. The set should be a quiet one with the subject and maybe the background music only to be heard.
- The audio should be monitored with a set of headphones while rehearsing and recording. There should be no rooms for any assumption.
- Practice zooming until perfection. When you zoom in or out, you should not be too fast or too slow else your video might appear too

amateurish. Practice the art of zooming until you reach a stage where you know your capabilities and that of the camcorder.

- Extra seconds should be shot at the start and end. With the extra seconds, you have a better level of freedom while editing the video.

The focus of the video should be on the subject and not on anything else. Therefore, technical hitches should not be entertained at all.

USE TWO CAMERAS

It is mind-blowing what can be achieved with a single good camera. It is even more fascinating what can be achieved when two cameras are put into good use. Depending on your financial strength, two good cameras are better to be used in shooting than one. It adds a professional spice to the video. With one camera directly facing the subject, and another shooting from a different angle, the video is way better. This also allows you to cut between shots whilst editing thereby offering variety in the video. Using two cameras also makes it easier for you to edit the speaker should the need arise.

LOOK PROFESSIONAL- OR NOT

Fashion designers often give a particular advice; make sure to dress for the occasion. Let us picture a scenario. A 100-metre sprint athlete preparing to participate in a championship heats casually dressed in his suits, ties and expensive pair of shoes. The athlete would not be taken seriously as he is over dressed for the occasion. In the same vein, every video should have a particular look depending on the target audience and the message been passed across. When you are representing a professional business, your video has to look professional. When you are giving out a hip young vibe, consider putting on casual personal wears that exude the age. In summary, make sure that your video has a look and feel that matches your brand's message.

CONSIDER CREATING A SLIDESHOW

New entrants to the YouTube scene who may not have the financial wherewithal to pull off fascinating videos may wish to employ the services of a slideshow. It involves compiling many still photos into a slide with the addition of a background music or voiceover. This is low budget and can be used in some topics that require PowerPoint presentations.

HIRE A PROFESSIONAL

No one is an Island. There is a never a Jack of all trades. Perhaps you do not have the necessary expertise or resources to produce your own video. What you need do is to employ the services of professionals in the field. You may learn a thing from them in the process. You may wish to employ the services of students in the film department as they will definitely charge lower.

BREAK THE RULES

There is no one way of doing things. At any point you feel you can achieve the best results in your videos by going against the 'normal' rules, feel free to break them. What matters is the result at the end. Always trust your instincts in taking calculated risks. In essence, do whatever it takes to achieve the effect you want.

BE ENTERTAINING

In creating content for YouTube, your aim is to make your viewers come back for more and perhaps share the video with others. The central rule of any YouTube content is that it must be entertaining. When you produce a boring video, you might just be the only person that will watch it. People always want to be entertained so you must give them what they want at all times. Nobody wants to know how boring the products you are selling are, you have to find a way of making the video entertaining. Humour sells products so it should be taken into cognizance. Your viewers should at the least see the video entertaining as to watch through the entire length.

BE INFORMATIVE

If you are not informed, you become deformed. Don't ask me where I got that quote from! I am pretty sure I saw it in one those countless motivational books out there but I don't seem to recall the particular one though. Your videos being entertaining is essential, but being informative is even more essential. There should be valid information passed across by each video. The aim of any video has been defeated if it lacks information. A video should be useful information presented to the viewers in an entertaining manner. The entertainment lure people in no doubts, but they stay only because of the information.

GO FOR THE FUNNY

We already established that videos need to be entertaining. Is there a better way to be entertaining aside being funny? An average person wants to laugh and will always remember memories of laughter. People will always remember the funny videos they watched on YouTube and the probability of their sharing with others is high. Humorous videos always go viral in contrast to their overly serious counterparts. You should never take yourself or your brand too seriously. Always make jokes and laugh genuinely. People know when it is faked. When you laugh at yourself, the audience will certainly laugh with you. That way, an emotional connection is built.

THE SHORTER, THE BETTER

Performing actors are often taught to leave the stage when the ovation is loudest. When your video is too long, the entertainment in it starts waning off. The average viewer does not want to spend more than a few minutes of his time on your never-ending video. It is interesting to note that even a three- minute video has trouble holding viewer's attention. It is therefore advised to keep your videos very short and at the same time pass the message across. There should be no beatings about the bush. Some experts say five minutes is ideal for videos, some agree on 20 seconds, yet others believe 3 minutes should do it. Whatever be the case, the message in the video should be passed quickly and efficiently. The shorter, the better! In the case of topics that require more than a few minutes to discuss, you may wish to break the videos into parts and upload differently.

KEEP IT SIMPLE/ STAY FOCUSED

It is not the amount you spend in producing videos that make it effective. You do not need to spend a lot of fortune in producing one video when someone speaking directly to a camera can do the trick. One major way of keeping it simple is by staying focused on a single message. You should never forget that time economy is key. You do not have to start introducing all the products in one video, nobody would watch it. A video should be dedicated to a particular product or message.

ALWAYS COMMUNICATE A CLEAR MESSAGE

It does not matter the type of video you are uploading on YouTube. If people cannot in two words tell you what the video is all about, then, the video has failed. Viewers need to have a clear idea of what the video is all about and its relevance to them.

CHAPTER 7
UPLOADING VIDEOS

We are gradually getting to the business end of the book. Once that video gets out onto the web, it will either soar or crash. Assuming you shot your video with a camcorder. It is expected you should have long transferred the video from the camcorder to your computer's hard drive, where the necessary editing should take place. The final best possible video is what you upload to YouTube. To select a video file for upload, some prerequisites should be met. The video must be in a YouTube-approved format, the video has to be less than 15 minutes long. It also has to be smaller than 2GB in size. So long as the requirements are met, you are ready to upload. It should be noted that uploaded videos should not contain any copyrighted content, such as music playing in the background. Since YouTube is potentially for all consumers, there should be no adult content in all videos uploaded. That's by the way.

To get the video upload started;

- The **upload link** near the right corner of any YouTube page should be clicked. It displays the **Video File Upload Page**. To continue with the upload, the **Upload Video** button is clicked.
- Upon clicking, the **Select File(s)to upload window** is seen. This is where you navigate to and select the desired video file you want to upload with the **Open button** clicked.

YouTube takes it up from here in uploading the selected file. The upload depending on the file size and the internet signal strength might take some time. It might even linger on for several minutes over a poor internet connection bearing in mind that there is an additional processing time where YouTube converts the uploaded video to its own format and adds it to its database.

It is one thing to upload a very good video to YouTube and another thing entirely to get people see what you have embedded in the video. That been said, it is safe to say then that what makes videos sell is the information around or about it. When even the best video has poor information in form of description, people will certainly deem it is as poor as the description.

We will be laying emphasis on certain information that promote the video and make it appealing to the viewers. They include;

- Thumbnails
- Title
- Description
- Tags
- Category
- Privacy
- Sharing options

THUMBNAILS

These refer to display images that YouTube assigns to each video on its site. These images are what the viewers see on the YouTube's video search results; viewers also see these images on a producer's channel page, and everywhere on the site. Thumbnail is the face of the uploaded video. The responsibility of choosing the images which appear as thumbnails lie on you and you alone. During the uploading process, when the bulk of the video has been uploaded, YouTube automatically selects five images from the video that can serve as the thumbnail. It is left for you to decide on the one that fits the position perfectly by clicking on it. However, in some cases, the potential thumbnail images are not shown until the video has been fully uploaded. It is advised to choose the image that best describes the goal of the video.

TITLE

Can we ever over emphasize this concept? The answer is a definite no! The title is the first thing that draws the viewer to the video. When the title is wrong, the video is wrong, the whole process is wrong. Absolute care should be taken when choosing the title of the video. The title should be able to describe the video in very few words. It should never be overly long. In fact, the title should be as catchy as an advertising headline. It should be catchy, straight to the point and short.

DESCRIPTION

This should be seen as the bigger or longer title. This is the ultimate selling point of the video. It should contain all the information the viewer needs to have of the video. The description can and should be longer than the traditional title. A good description should be able to trigger viewers to ask for more information or directly purchase whatever you are selling without questions. It should also contain your personal information should the viewer have any need of reaching you. Such personal information may include;

- Personal website address
- E-mail address
- Telephone number
- Postal mailing address

There should not be any room for being overly polite in the description. Any information you think the viewer will find relevant should be included no matter how stupid or foolish it might look to you. You are in for the money after all.

TAGS

Tags are as important as the title and description. They are those keywords the viewer inputs in the search area of the site for your video to pop up. Therefore, a tag is another name for a keyword. In choosing tags, you are saddled with two heavy responsibilities; thinking for yourself and thinking for the viewers. In thinking for yourself, you are the content creator therefore you know the goal you are out to achieve with the video so you use keywords that align with the problem the video is solving. Nevertheless, in thinking for the viewers, you are saddled with the onerous task of thinking just the same way your viewers would when typing in words that would bring your video to their screens. Tags can be as many as possible. The rule is just that each tag should be separated from the other by a space. Probable words you feel the viewer would search for when looking for your video should only be used as tags. Your tags should include your company names, it should include the topic of the video, and every other descriptive word or phrase.

CATEGORY

Category is to YouTube what genre is to literature and music. A jazz musician can never identify as a blues artiste. If he ever does so, he will only be misleading the public and will eventually pay with drop in patronage and sales. In the same vein, any video uploaded to YouTube should be evenly matched to the most appropriate category. That is the only way viewers will be able to identify it easily from the YouTube search engine. Let us imagine a scenario where a football pundit analyses a high profile football match and mistakenly or purposely decides to place the video in the fashion category of YouTube. What do you think will become of the video? Your thought is as good as mine. The video will not be seen by most people in the football world irrespective of the high content because it is wrongly categorized. It is advised that you select the category that best fits your video from the pull-down list. The categories in YouTube in alphabetical order include;

- Autos & Vehicles
- Comedy
- Education
- Entertainment
- Film & Animation
- Gaming
- How to & Style
- Music
- News & Politics
- Non-profits & Activism
- People & Blogs
- Pets & Animals
- Science & Technology
- Sports
- Travel & Events.

PRIVACY

This is where you determine who gets to see your video. There are three options of people who can view your video, they are;

- Public

- Unlisted
- Private

In the public option, anyone on YouTube can search for and view the video. It is ideal for businesses that do not have a specific age bracket as target customers.

In the unlisted option, only those viewers who know the link to the video can view it. This option is very selective.

In the private option, only the people invited by the user can view the video. The private option is suitable for private presentations that the user may wish to share with a selected few.

SHARING OPTIONS

The sharing option section is located at the bottom of the Video File Upload Page. This is where the URL of the video uploaded is found. The HTML code of the video can also be found here. These HTML code and URL are used in embedding the video to another web page.

CUSTOM URLs

First off, URL is an acronym for Uniform Resource Locator. It is used by browsers to retrieve any published content in the web. URL just like HTTP is a very key component of the web. A YouTube custom URL is therefore a simple and personalized channel URL that can be shared to the viewers of a channel. You may be wondering at this point of what essence it is customize the URL since it will still be the same format. The answer is simple. YouTube generates a default URL for its users but the URL generated may not be enticing to you talk more of your viewers. Typical YouTube URLs are very lengthy and most times does not have any relationship with the content it aims to share; you do not want to be sharing that with your audience. You should be thinking of how to make life easier for your viewers and not the other way round. YouTube seems to know that their URLs would not be the ultimate by offering channels the ability to set their own URL so long as a few requirements set to make you eligible are met.

The eligibility requirements include;

- A channel seeking to customize its URL must have a hundred (100) or more subscribers.
- The channel should be at least 30 days old. That's a month approximately. YouTube wants to make sure that you are here to stay.
- There should be a profile picture uploaded in your channel
- There has to be a banner image uploaded.

There is no way you will be able to customize your URL without first attaining the above mentioned heights. There have been arguments that custom URL are not actually 'custom'. This is because YouTube also plays a role in the selection of the 'custom' URL. It plays this role by suggesting available options based on: Username, display name, linked website name, and current vanity URLs. However, YouTube does this to tailor URLs to the channels they are sharing. However, you can manipulate YouTube's suggestions by setting your username and other available options to something you would like your URL to be. That way, YouTube just suggests what you already want to use.

The steps taken to set a custom YouTube channel URL are;

- Sign in to YouTube studio. There is no way you will be able to drive a vehicle without first starting the ignition. In this scenario, creating a custom URL is the car you want to drive; you have to sign in to YouTube studio, which is the ignition you have to turn on.

- When inside the YouTube studio, select **Customization**, and then also select **Basic Info**
- A Channel URL heading should be visible to you at this juncture, select the **Set a custom URL for your channel.** This is where YouTube opens a box for you to see the customized URLs it has suggested to you, based on your channel details. An option of adding extra numbers and letters to further aid the customization is also given.
- Click on the **Confirm custom URL** and you have your personalized URL ready for sharing to the viewers.

CHAPTER 8
PREMIERING A VIDEO

YouTube is a site that knows that people always want more. Therefore, it keeps thriving on innovation to meet up with the never ending demands of the digital age we are in. One of their numerous ways of keeping up with this trend is by launching the YouTube Premieres. It is a feature that lets you and your viewers watch and actually feel the thrills of a new video together in real time. Premiering a video creates vibes around videos. It is also a means of hyping and promoting a video. However, where is the fun of premiering a video when you end up being the only one that gets to eventually watch it? The buzz is created when the watch page is shared to the viewers. This informs them ahead of time thereby affording those amongst them who may wish to watch the video ample time to set reminders, leave comments and the likes. An interesting way of even adding more sauce to the fun is by guiding your viewers to video premiere using a live stream. It is worthy of note that some videos are not supported for premieres. They include videos of

360/vr180 or those whose output are greater than 1080p.

When a premiere is created, YouTube is tasked with creating a public watch page for you. The watch page is where your video will premiere on. It is advised to share the watch page URL with the public to attract even more viewers. A video premiere can be watched on all the available platforms such as the computer, Android and the likes and should be used to your full advantage. Chatting with viewers on the watch page before and even during the premiere is recommended by YouTube as it helps in promoting your premiere. To create a premiere, a few detailed steps should be religiously heeded. They include;

- Go to www.studio.Youtube.com on your computer.
- You then click on the **Upload videos** link. The link is easily located at the top of the page. There should be no difficulties locating it.

- The video to be uploaded is selected. This is where you also enter the details of the video.
- You may wish to premiere the video instantly or schedule for later. If you are premiering immediately, then, click on **Save or publish**, click on **Public**, and the non **Instant premiere**. As soon as the video is done processing, it premieres. When scheduling for a later time, click on **Schedule, Enter a date and time** (this is where you choose the date and time you want the video to premiere), then on **Set as premiere**.
- Finally, click on **Done** or **Schedule**.

Nevertheless, there is an alternative means of creating a premiere for users of the YouTube app. When uploading videos from the app, simply go to the **Set visibility** page, and choose **Set as Premiere**. Now is that not simple?

With the premiere over, the video remains on the channel page as a regular upload. Did we mention that the premiere can only be done a desktop? Yes, you heard correctly.

GOING LIVE ON YOUTUBE

Given that most YouTube videos are pre-recorded, it rips off the interactive experience that many would have liked. Viewers who perhaps are not deeply satisfied with what they have just seen on the video and would like to ask questions are left to vent their frustrations off as comments in the comment section. There is an improvement on that limitation, offered also on a platter of gold as it is absolutely free. YouTube live has changed the narratives. It has transformed the before-now boring online non-interactive video sessions into lively interactive experiences. With the enormous hours of video uploaded to YouTube every minute, users are constantly in a competition to have their videos watched. Streaming live when done right might just that way of standing out from the crowd and drawing the traffic to your videos. The keyword in the statement above is 'when done right'. This is because when live streams are done in not so good ways, it could as well ultimately sink your YouTube ship.

To go live on YouTube, you have to enable your channel. To have your channel enabled, it needs to be verified. To verify your channel is a simple task as you just have to go to www.youtube.com/verify and add your phone number. A verification code will be sent to your phone number as a confirmation. On receiving the confirmation text from YouTube, if you are using a desktop computer;

- Go to www.youtube.com/dashboard.
- The **Create button** in the top right corner should be clicked.
- **Go live** should be selected.

The minimum time it takes to activate your live streaming account barring any internet connection hitch is 24 hours.

For mobile phone users,

- Scroll to and open the YouTube app.
- The **camcorder icon** in the top right corner should be clicked.
- Then tap **Go live**.

Mobile live streaming does not come easy. This is because as a mobile user, you need to have more than a thousand (1,000) subscribers to live stream.

In a bid to save the planet some paper, live stream creation on YouTube will be limited to desktop and mobile devices only in this book.

To create a YouTube live stream on desktop;

- Using a supported browser, go to the default YouTube page www.youtube.com/dashboard.
- The **camcorder icon** in the top right corner should be clicked.
- **Go live** should be clicked, with **Webcam** selected.
- Add the title you want and adjust the privacy settings to taste.
- The **More options** should be clicked. This is where you add a description, enable or disable live chat, select monetization option and so on.
- Click **Next**. On clicking, YouTube takes a thumbnail photo of you. You may wish to retake the photo until the desired image is gotten. You

may also wish to upload an image from your hard disk.

- And.....Action! Select **Go live** to get the action started.
- When you are done, select **End Stream** at the bottom.

To create a YouTube live stream on mobile;

- Scroll to and select the camcorder icon from the YouTube app.
- Then select **Go live**.
- The title and privacy setting should be added.
- The **More Options** should be selected. You add a description to the live stream here. Then select **Show More** to enable or disable live chats. Age restriction, monetization options and more can also be set here.
- Press the **Show Less** to exit, then select **Next**. You then take a picture or upload an existing image as thumbnail.

- You then tap the **Share**. It shares the link to your other social media accounts.
- And..... Action! Tap **Go live** to get the action started.
- Tap **Finish** and then **Ok** to end the live stream.

SOME TIPS FOR OPTIMIZING THE YOUTUBE LIVE

- The basics and Intent should be well prepared. You do not set up a live stream only to start acting confused mid-air. You should know the reason you are setting up in the first place. The goal of the live stream should never be defeated. Before the **Go live** is clicked, ensure that everything is in order. The intent of making a live video as opposed to a regular video should be buttressed in the video. Make sure the viewers do not get bored throughout the show by ensuring you offer a well packaged content. You should also have your call to action (what you want the viewer doing during and after the live stream) ready.

- Choose the near-perfect time. It is understood that there can never be a perfect time for everyone to be online. The aim therefore should be to choose a time when majority of your viewers will be online. YouTube analytics comes into play here; you can check when your previous videos usually get the most views. This should clearly show you that they are often online at that time. You may also decide to check the locations of your viewers. This helps you in choosing a time that will be favourable in multiple time zones. However, the surest way to know the best time is to ask the audience. You can achieve this by creating a poll in the social media where viewers choose their suitable time in the comment section.
- Use the best equipment/ check setup. Can this ever be overemphasized? Going live has its own fair share of disadvantages. One of it being that a mistake can never be edited once it is live. It will be disastrous and embarrassing that you spent one

hour streaming live only to discover that the microphones were not working properly after the whole show. It may sound funny but it is very possible. As a preventive measure to similar situations, the best equipment should be used to get the best possible content. Other setup such as the audio, lighting and the likes should be properly checked beforehand likewise. Also ensure to stay connected to a power source to avoid battery failures.

- Promote the event well. What's the point of going live again? To have an audience you can interact with I suppose. If you then go live and there is no audience, you are dead on arrival. You have to work for this audience. Nothing good comes easy after all. The best bet to getting them is through promotion. There are various outlets for promotion and they should be treated seriously. You can start by designing a banner that promotes the event for your channel. You can also run the YouTube live stream display ads that promote videos. Another effective way of promoting the live stream is by sharing your streaming link on other social media handles at least 48 hours before going live with specific details. You can also send invitations via email.

- Actively engage the audience. Now, you have done the hard part, you have run the promotions. It was successful and you have setup and gone live. Your audience is patiently gazing at you to hear what you have to say. A majority of them will actually run out of patience and zoom off if you go on talking and talking. You have to keep them there. However, when the audience are actively engaged in the discourse, they will always want to see out the interesting session. Be sure to provide recaps at intervals as people might be joining even as the streaming is going on. You do not want them to come in, get confused and hit the roads immediately. Another ploy that keeps the audience glued to their screens is the anticipation you have built over the streaming. Always give the audience a good reason to want to see to the end of the session. There should be some air of suspense throughout the show. Furthermore, the viewers should be told they are seen. Shout out names or usernames intermittently. The viewer feels connected when he hears his name shouted out. Love, just like respect is reciprocal. The viewers should be allowed to participate actively in the live chat. This way, they are actively engaged and post comments based on the matter on ground.

CHAPTER 9

TRACKING YOUR CHANNEL'S GROWTH

Anyone can decide to create a YouTube channel and upload videos, it is free after all. Only a few however, see it to grow the channel and make money from it perhaps because of the hassle that comes with it eventually. Students in a school from time to time are given assignments, tests and examinations. These parameters serve as a yardstick which helps the teacher in knowing or measuring the depth of the students' understanding. The same approach is applied in YouTube. To judge how effective your videos are, there is a need to track how your channel is doing in terms of general views and all other whatnots. Luckily enough, YouTube provides some metrics you can use to track their performances. One may ask, why should I track my videos? I have played my own part in making and uploading them after all. There are a host of valid reasons why keeping track of your videos are important- very important. You track the performance of your videos so as to be able to fine-tune your activities to have bigger impact. You track to measure the effectiveness of your efforts, and to learn from your previous efforts in planning future activities.

TRACKING TO FINE-TUNE YOUR EFFORTS

Students in the schools do not have to wait until the end of the school session before they are hit with tests or examinations; the mid-session tests are always there to check progress along the line. This test helps the teacher in knowing for sure the areas of his craft he needs to fine-tune before the end of the session. In the same vein, a YouTube channel owner does not have to wait until the end of a given campaign to track its performance. It sounds and feels better looking at the scenario as it is playing out. This will help in making any mid-course correction that might arise.Tracking your performances periodically and positively adjusting the wrong aspects makes the overall output even greater.

TRACKING TO MEASURE EFFECTIVENESS

Marketing teaches that before you set out to any campaign, you need to have a measurable goal. There should also be a strategic plan on how to achieve the goal. That been said, at the end of any given campaign, there is a need to measure how effective it was. You still remember the end of session examinations right? What were its goals then? You guessed correctly again. It is there to measure how effective you were as a student during the course of the session. Most if not all students set near impossible goals that they wish to achieve by the end of the session. While some may wish to ace all their courses, some others may want to attain a certain cumulative grade point and so more. With the examinations written and results published, the student can now measure how effective his goals for the session were met. This is achieved by placing the initial goal alongside the results that were obtained. The same approach should be applied to YouTube. Set goals of a certain amount of viewership before any upload and thereafter measure the actual views against the expected views. It helps in analysing performances.

TRACKING TO PLAN FUTURE ACTIVITIES

We will agree that the past and present help in shaping the future. Mistakes can do only two things to an event- make or mar. When a mistake is made in the past, if the person involved views it from a positive light, analyses it and puts it into practice, the mistake will most likely not happen again. Bringing it over your YouTube career, we are assuming that your previous uploaded video did not get the expected views. You need to find out for certain why it did so and then apply the knowledge to the next video production. You cannot be repeating the same mistakes over and over again. On the other hand, if the video gathered views even above the expected margin, then, the success hints should also be incorporated in the future projects. Every activity should serve a purpose. There should be a lesson in both failure and success. The experiences gathered from the first video should shape how the second one should be. The experiences gathered from the second should shape the third and so on.

VIEWS, RATINGS AND COMMENTS TRACKING

The important metrics for measuring or tracking the above are located directly below the video player on the video page.

VIEWS The most important metric is arguably the views number. You basically upload your video so that people watch. If it hasn't been watched after uploading or the views are not good enough, then just maybe some things are not right. It is quite hard to say for sure the number of views that are good enough for a particular video. But then, when a video generates views raking in millions in a day or even less, doesn't it scream awesomeness? Some videos however might be doing fine even with a 100 views. Such videos are professional business videos that target a much selected few. Nevertheless, it has been proven over the years that raw views can be a false measurement. For the singular fact that your video has been viewed doesn't automatically mean that the goal you are out to achieve has been accomplished. A music sales video which generated over a million views probably because of its entertaining content but sold no single music copy will not be regarded as successful.

LIKES AND DISLIKES JUDGEMENT

This thumbs up/ thumbs down feature, is another way a viewer may rate a video. It's a thumb up if they like it and a thumb down if the reverse is the case. It is needless to say that the more liked video is obviously the better. The total number of the 'likes' against 'dislikes' is graphed on a button underneath the video. It is recommended that you visit the graph to see things for yourself always.

COMMENTS The comment left by viewers on the videos is also another important metric for tracking performance. These comments constitute a source of useful feedback from the audience who have watched the video. Personally, the number of comments matter more to me than the number of views. Anybody can just take click the like button, but it takes something special for one to hold on a while longer and actually comment. It shows a level of engagement in the video. When the number of comments is high, it then means that you engaged the viewer actively throughout the video. The content of the comments on the other hand tells you what the viewer likes or dislikes in the video.

USING GOOGLE ANALYTICS We have established the importance of tracking before now. With Google analytics, your channel and video performance can be monitored with real time metrics and reports on your YouTube analytics page. There are a variety of options to choose from but the study will be limited to the overview report, revenue report, ad rates report, watch time, engagement report, real-time reports, and demographic reports.

To get started using the analytic tools, you can directly go through the www.youtube.com/analytics or the detailed steps below should be followed.

- First, sign into your YouTube account, then click the **Creator studio** icon.
- On the left side, select **Analytics**.
- This is where you choose the report you want to see as there are many of them.

We will now attempt to analyse the various reports that can be accessed from YouTube analytics and their relationship to the popularity and performance of your videos and channel in general.

THE OVERVIEW REPORT

This can be said to be a high-level summary of how your contents are faring on YouTube. According to YouTube, it should be used to ascertain some basic performance features for your YouTube content. The performance metrics, engagement metrics, top 10 content, demographics and discovery sections are all enclosed in the overview report.

The Performance metrics is tasked with the summary of watch time, views and the earnings of the selected content.

The Engagement metrics deals with displaying the most relevant data for the engagement criteria. Such criteria include likes, comments, dislikes, favourites and shares.

Top 10 content as the name imply shows you the top 10 content pieces for your channel.

Demographics is tasked with information gathering on the gender and location of viewers. This lets the user know the locations with the highest viewership of his contents. It also opens your eyes to the age bracket that view your content the most. This ultimately helps you in creation of other videos as you now know your target audience.

Discovery gives the summary for top playback locations and top traffic sources by watch time. This means that you get to know where most of the traffic is coming from in specific times of the video.

REVENUE REPORTS

This report is not available for all the users of YouTube. It is only available to YouTube partners who have an associated Adsense account.

To see the revenue report;

- You have to first log in to your YouTube account.

- Just as in the previous case, select your account and then Creator studio at the top right.
- Click on **Analytics**, then **Revenue Report** in the left menu

The revenue report is used to see all revenue-related details at the channel and the video levels. It shows the revenue derived from transactions such as paid content, the revenue derived from YouTube Red. It also shows the net revenue from all Google-sold advertising sources for any selected date range and region and so much more. In essence, the revenue reports show you all the revenue related reports you can ever imagine on YouTube.

AD RATES REPORT

Just like the revenue reports, the Ad rate report is only available for YouTube partners who have access to revenue data in their account. It is interested with the advertisement rates and payment of channels. This report provides information on ad revenue, monetized playbacks and the likes. The report is used to access how different types of adverts are performing over time. In summary, it shows the amount advertisers paid to run an advert in your channel. It does not necessarily mean that the money is yours entirely.

To access the Ads rates report;

- Log in to your YouTube account.
- Select your account and then **Creator studio** at the top right.
- Click on **Analytics**, then **Ad rates** in the left menu.

WATCH TIME REPORT

This particular report helps in the production of future content for the YouTube audience. It is a report that helps the content creator to understand how well different videos engage the viewers. It does not only cover the watch time as the name implies. It covers many other facets of the video.These include the average view duration, audience retention, and average percentage viewed reports. These metrics are used to get into the minds of the viewers from how engaged they were in the previous videos. This helps in knowing how to get them interested in watching more of your videos. The audience retention report helps you know how well the videos you upload keep its audience. Do they stay up to the end of the video? Do they run off when the video is still in play? This report answers these questions. The Playback location report shows all the sites or WebPages your videos are being viewed on. Now, doesn't this sound interesting? Traffic sources report helps you when promotions for the next video. This is so because it shows all the available sites and YouTube features that your viewers use to find your content. When you have this information, it even pushes you to add more effort promoting subsequent videos in those outlets. Device reports show you the different operating systems and devices being used to watch your videos by viewers. The demographics is a graph-like report that helps one in understanding the gender distribution and age range of your audience. This information is generated from the logged-in viewers from all the available devices.

CHAPTER 10
CHANNEL PROMOTION

Just recently, it was all over the news that YouTube had overtaken Facebook as the most visited site on the web. Is the reason enough to get you want to promote your YouTube channel or do you still have to wait until it clinches the first position? Chances are there that by then, it might not be free as it is now though. We are in an age of video consumption. Mastering the art of channel promotion will most definitely put your channel on the screens of everyone surfing YouTube. Growing massive audience on YouTube does not happen by chance or accident. This chapter aims to divulge all the ways you can take advantage of as many promotional tactics as possible. We have also taken into account that you are still as a starter; these tips are all fair game still.

1. Use engaging, descriptive titles:

YouTube is basically marketing with videos. It is all about the presentation. Since the title is the first thing viewers see when they search for your content, you do not want to keep them boring. A boring title is a pointer to a boring video. Titles are deal breakers when it comes to video performances. Engaging, eye catchy, must-see, descriptive titles make videos whereas boring titles mar videos. You want to grab your audience's attention from the word 'go'.

In order to write strong YouTube titles, the following tips should be considered.

- It should be sweet and short. The trick is that the shorter is always the better in YouTube. Nobody wants to read epistles on YouTube; they are here to watch videos after all. When the title is long then, it's already a turn off. Limit your titles to 60 characters or even less. If you insist on displaying your long writing prowess in your titles, you should also be ready to see some part of your title cut off by YouTube when displayed. It is advised you take your time in choosing a befitting title instead of rushing and killing everything off with an awful title. You don't have to choose the first idea that comes to mind.

- Insert keyword(s) in the first part of the title. Viewers are on YouTube to watch videos and not to read. Most of them just read the first few lines and either click to play the video or hit the roads immediately. Ensure you place the interesting keyword(s) that have the information to grab the viewer's attention in the first few lines.
- Do not use click baits. Inasmuch as you want to create an emotional reaction in the minds of the viewers, you should not offer click baits as headlines. When your channel is tagged a hub of click bait titles, your career in YouTube is as good as over.
- You may as well employ the services of YouTube's auto complete feature if you are not sure of the title to choose. You can search a particular topic in

the feature and check out the popular keywords the feature gives you.

2. Choose SEO and Google-friendly keywords. SEO is an acronym that stands for search engine optimization. From the name alone, it is safe to say that they are those words that are likely to pop up when people are searching the web. We have not forgotten that YouTube is also a part of the web, have we? As it is, viewers do not just search for videos on YouTube alone, they also search on Google. If you are having issues conjuring up good words, you can try the "How to" or "tutorial" words since they are already widely used. It is advised that you choose a keyword that spotlight videos. In the same vein, use keywords that suit your content. As an example, if you are to search for "Piano playing tutorial" and "Piano Playing tips" on Google, you will notice that "Piano playing tutorial" will turn up far more

results than "Piano playing tips". The same scenario is still likely to pan out in YouTube search.

3. Fill out your profile completely. Most times, content creators neglect to fill out the profile section. They just jump straight into the business of producing and uploading videos. They do so mainly out of ignorance because had they known the importance of an outstanding profile, they would have attended to it before any other thing. A filled out outstanding profile remains one of the easiest ways of promoting the YouTube channel. It also helps in boosting of ones SEO. When filling your profile;

- Be sure to be consistent in using similar features as with your website and other social media accounts for easy identification.

- Make sure to include your contact information. Some of your viewers may want to reach you for partnerships and the likes. Make it easy for them.
- Your fans should know when to expect new stuff. Stick religiously to it to boost your credibility.
- Make the best use of your YouTube channel description. Hope you still remember what we said about keywords earlier? Apply them here likewise.

4. Offer real value.

On YouTube, there is one Texas piano teacher Shawn Cheek popularly known as Shawn cheek easy. His videos also rank among the highest on the list of the Most Subscribed Gurus. In one of his interviews, the piano tutor had this to say on YouTube, "To be successful on YouTube you have to do two things: Provide something that people want and do it in a way that no one else is doing it. There are tons of piano lessons to be had on YouTube, but no one uses the method that I use, at least not yet! One other thing: I read every response that I get and try to provide lessons that most people ask for. When people hear back from you, when they know that you are there, that's when you really build a following".Therefore, always seek to add value to people in any video you are uploading. Do not just upload for the sake of uploading. Before uploading a video, ask yourself some questions: The video I am about uploading, how entertaining is it? Does it solve any problem? If yes, what are the problems? Will the video ultimately improve the lives of the viewers in any positive way? When these questions are all answered honestly before uploading, then, wait for the magic.

5. Upload high quality videos. Videos of low quality will stand no chance of competing with those of high qualities irrespective of the high contents. Ensure your video has attained a certain degree of professionalism before posting. If you are going live, ensure to do your proper sound checks before hitting the Go live button. However, it is still not a crime if you are not versed in video production, you can pay others to do it for you while you concentrate on being the star of the show.
6. Have a hearty interaction with the fans. We often do not know the value of what we have until we lose it or at the very point of losing it. You are not paying anyone to be your subscriber or your fan. Always take out time to constantly monitor and interact with them. It is the least you could ever do for them. Make it a point of duty to respond to all

their comments- the negative ones inclusive. There is always a lesson to be learnt in all of them. Make use of the YouTube analytics tools to get to know your huge fans and always show them love.

7. A Question & Answer adds spice. This is an effective way of building up a community. You may wish to ask viewers to send questions they want addressed through your social media channels, email, or even through the comment section. A video is then dedicated to answering all of the questions. Question and answer sessions show fans a sense of belonging. It shows them that you see them, that they truly matter. The fans will always reward your little act of love by sticking around to watch your videos. Some might also go the extra length of sharing your channel to other friends.
8. Be active with the YouTube community. That you are a channel owner does not make you an island. Remember that YouTube is about finding your passion and building on it. Therefore, always

search for and subscribe to channels that share a similar idea to yours. Always watch their content, like and even share them. Show the kind of love you want shown to you. Leave encouraging comments and if possible go the extra length of acknowledging them in your own videos. Be assured that the kind gesture would not go unnoticed. They will get to notice and reciprocate the action one of these days and it can only result in one thing- getting new viewers. Engage with the YouTube community the much you can.

9. Collaborate with other YouTubers/ brands. When one is running a monopolized channel, there are chances that he may run out of ideas at a given stage. However, the probability of him running out of ideas if he has partners is very low. Two or more good heads will always be better than one. Working with other youtubers/ brands also broadens ones horizons into achieving heights he could never think of prior. Nevertheless, you

should not sacrifice your authenticity on the altar of collaboration. Look for and partner with youtubers/ brands who share a similar vision. Collaborate with brands that share your values. It is better not to collaborate at all than to collaborate and go against your values and those of your viewers. The backlash will be detrimental.

10. Cross-promotion draws traffic. Bearing in mind that YouTube is only 'one' site out of the numerous others that exist, strategize on ways of reaching out to people outside of it to further build your channel. Your videos should be incorporated into social media accounts, blogs, and the likes since everyone might not be seeing you on YouTube. With the exposure and the link shared therein, with a single click, viewers are redirected to your YouTube channel.

11. Do more of what works. We dedicated a section of this book to YouTube analytics because of its relevance to the study. It should be a reliable guide to you. Always fall back to it when things

start looking confusing. Make it a faithful companion in the journey. There is no other way you know what your viewers want, or how they feel, or their age group, or their location, the languages they speak, and importantly the type of videos they prefer if not through analytics. It should be used wisely and optimally. When you have found out what works for them, do it more. You are creating the videos for them after all; it is not for your personal consumption.

12. Consider running contests and giveaways. This is better done using live interactions. It is a way of spicing things up and getting the viewer more involved. YouTube contests and giveaways encourage people to subscribe to your channel and engage. The contest should be promoted on other social media accounts, blogs, newsletters, emails and the likes to bring in a large audience base. The aim of the activity is still to promote the channel remember? You should take note of the

following though before going ahead with the contest.

- Clear Goal. There should be a clear goal behind running the contest. In this case, the goal is to promote the channel by bringing in more viewers/ subscribers. The goal should always be in mind and must never be defeated.
- YouTube has contest rules and restrictions. You must respect them.
- The prize to be given to the winner(s) should be a prize the viewers would actually enjoy. If possible, depending on your financial strength, present options to the viewers to choose from. It will make them feel more involved.

However, after running each contest, always have a look at the analytics to ascertain the effects on the subscriber drop-off rate and engagements. If the statistics are encouraging, you may have to host another contest anytime soon but if the results are the other way round, you should stop as it looks as though you are wasting your resources to no gain whatsoever.

13. Customize and optimize your thumbnails. This is one of the easiest yet effective means of promoting the YouTube channel. It is an almost generally accepted fact that first impressions really matter in situations. The title and the thumbnail are the first impressions to any content in your channel; they deserve to be used effectively. YouTube by default generates a screenshot from an uploaded content and uses it for the thumbnail. What then happens when the image it grabs is a not-so good one? Do you resign yourself to fate and watch your efforts in the video production washed down the drains? I wouldn't. It is possible to create your own thumbnails on YouTube. You may wish to do it yourself and optimize the image to promote your channel the more. Your thumbnail must be able to represent your brand and what the people think of your channel. People often go for those videos that

have a touch of professionalism in their thumbnails. The good news is that thumbnails are easily made with the help of image creation tools. *Canva* is a good example that can be used.

14. Create an interesting series. Creating interesting series is a sure way of promoting channels when done well. When viewers become attached to a particular series that air on a particular channel on certain days, they would surely tune in to watch. The content creator has it upon himself to search and engage in only very interesting topics that are sure to grab the viewer's attention. Your work is somewhat made easy as the content creator when you create a series as you do not have to rack your brain for fresh ideas as you just keep building on the already existing one. The viewers also have a worthwhile reason to always tune in to your channel.
15. Paid YouTube advertisement. Good businessmen always stress on the need it is to spend to gain. Is investment the right word? I think so. Depending

on the visibility you seek, doing away with a few bucks to paid YouTube ads is enough to propel your channel to higher heights. There are a host of ad formats to choose from: The display ads, overlay ads, skippable and non-skippable video ads, bumper ads, sponsored cards. You can choose from any of the advertising formats depending on what you can afford and the level of visibility that you seek. You can decide to use an existing video for a specific advertising campaign or create something new. Using an existing successful video can amplify the results of the advertisement. On the other hand, creating a new video for the advertisement allows you create a content that is better targeted towards what you want achieved.

16. Create Playlists to organize content. When you constantly buy new clothes without arranging the wardrobe, what happens, everywhere becomes scattered right? Look at the channel as the wardrobe in this case, with the uploaded videos as

the clothes. When the uploaded videos start getting too much, the channel just like the wardrobe tends to look unorganized or untidy. The remedy to the situation is by creating playlists. Playlists allow you to group the videos into categories thereby organizing the channel. These various playlists serve as guides to direct viewers to relevant content without having to search for ages.

17. Embedding videos direct the traffic. This works in directing traffic from other platforms to your YouTube channel. For instance, embedding your YouTube videos on your company's website is so great a way to introduce a new audience to your channel. If your personal website generates traffic, embedding your YouTube there could be a potential viewer driver. When tweeting or posting videos from your YouTube channel, ensure you do so in a playlist link so that viewers keep watching more videos.

CHAPTER 11
ENGAGING WITH VIEWERS

Communication involves two channels (the sender and the receiver). It is said to be ineffective when it flows to or from only one channel (sender). It is only complete when the two channels (sender and receiver) are involved. YouTube is an interactive platform. It is not an autocratic platform where only one party plays the role of the piper in dictating the tune others must dance to.

As soon as you start uploading and promoting your video, you start getting both appraisals and comments- negative ones inclusive. An appraisal would certainly encourage you and make you feel better. People always enjoy being told nice things. A negative comment from perhaps an internet troll on the other hand may make you feel bad. They are the two sides of the coin. A Gamer YouTube user MattShea, had someone he referred to as his 'biggest hater'. He went the extra length of creating a video to reply some of his questions and criticisms. The video was a hit. He got the hit from a negative comment situation. Trolling is quite common on social media these days, so it doesn't make sense feeding troll's trolling hunger. Comments should always be taken in positive lights and responded to softly.

The way you manage comments on your video is very important in engaging with your viewers. As no one is an island, some better learned viewers may have insights and suggestions that will add even more value to your videos. They may have questions that introduce different perspectives to the way you have been viewing situations. Therefore, how you manage your comments is a deal breaker in viewer engagement and the success of your YouTube career ultimately. It creates dialogue as it serves as the feedback that completes the communication process. Anyone viewing your video can by default leave comments about the video. But then, you are still the lord of your own space in YouTube as you can choose to disable comments, or choose to moderate comments before they appear publicly.

In controlling comments and video responses, you should click the down arrow closest to your name at the top of any YouTube page, and then select **My Videos** thereafter. This will display a list of all your videos. The **Edit button** should be clicked for the video you want to control. In the edit page, scroll down to the **Broadcasting and Sharing Options** section and adjust as you so desire. The options available on YouTube for accepting comments include;

- **Allow comments automatically**: This option allows all viewers to submit their text comments. These comments appear immediately on your video page. This option is not for the faint-hearted because online trolls may decide to take advantage and reel out myriads of negative comments.
- **Allow Friend comments automatically, all others with approval only**: This option allows all viewers to submit their text comments quite alright but

then, you would have to approve each comment before it appears on the video page. The only people whose comments will not require approvals are those who are part of your preapproved friends list.

- **Allow All Comments with approval only**: In this option, all the comments have to be approved before they are shown in the video page. Even those comments from your friends list need to be approved.
- **Don't Allow Comments**: In this option, the Comments section does not as much as appear on the page for this video.

The option to be chosen depends entirely on you. But then, how else do you hope to get feedback and actively engage your audience if not from the comment section. Choose wisely! There is always something to be learnt – from the negative comments especially.

DEALING WITH COMMENTS

So you have decided to allow viewers to leave comments on your videos. Be assured that you will surely receive useful comments from satisfied viewers which will make you happy and keep you going. However, you should also have it at the back of your mind that you will receive some negative comments- some of them might be very nasty. It is a fact that individuals accept things differently, some individuals want to see only positive comments. This is very fine but is it realistic in this world of ours? People have varying opinions. Opinions are bound to differ, that is what makes man unique. Since opinions differ, as you are getting positive comments, brace yourself for the nasty ones- they will surely find their way in.

Other individuals on the other hand, realize from the word go that there is no way they will have a 100% approval in anything they do. They are the realists. They are more open minded than the first category of individuals. They do not mind the negative comments. To them, the negative comments present the divergent opinions of people. You need to realize that man is insatiable.

Our concern now lies on how to deal with these negative comments because if it is not treated delicately, the effects might be bad.

- Removing them

For the faint-hearted, one cool way of dealing with a negative comment is by removing it. Chances are high that as you continue seeing the negative comment, you will not feel any better. To remove the comment then, simply go to the edit page for the particular video that has the comment and highlight the comment you want to remove. A number of new buttons are shown; the **Remove (trashcan) button** is your ally for the task you want to accomplish. With a single click on the Remove button, the comment goes into extinction.

- Blocking Specific Viewers

Some people just derive joy in seeing other people sad. They can go to any length to achieve this devilish aim. With the advent of internet and YouTube subsequently, their work has been made very easy for them. They can now hideaway behind the screens of their computers or internet enabled mobile devices to haunt others. These set of people will never post any positive comment. It will always be negative. Such people exist and a continued consumption of their negative comments might affect your other viewers. How do you deal with such person? You can manually remove all of his comments as soon as he posts them, but wouldn't that be too stressful for you? Why allow him post in the first place when you can kick him out already? YouTube developers already envisaged all these scenarios and provided the solutions beforehand. To block such individuals from leaving such negative comments and flooding your inbox with negativities all you have to do is click the member's name to access his channel. In his channel, scroll to the information box located above the user's profile. The **Block User link** is boldly situate there, do the needful! This user will never comment on your videos ever again nor contact you. Alternatively, if you are not the patient type like me, there is a way of blocking directly from the video where he must have commented negatively. There is usually a Block User button by the comment, **CLICK IT!**

- Face them head on!

The tough way of dealing with trolls is by facing them head-on, responding to their comments. YouTube allows a feature where you can as well add a response to any comments on your videos. It is meant to be an interaction area after all. To respond to comments, go to the video page. Scroll down to the comments section under the video window. You should see the list of all the viewer comments. Then highlight the comment to which you want to reply, click the **Reply button** and bingo!I assume you have decided to respond to the negative comments. I commend your courage for taking the bold step. Brace up for impact!

In responding to any comment- positive or negative, speed is very important. You need to respond when the conversation is still fresh. It shows the viewers that you take them seriously. That does not mean you respond with the first abusive word that comes to mind. Take a bit of time to digest the whole situation before responding as politely as possible. You need to stay positive in your response even to the nastiest of comments. Being polite doesn't necessarily mean not being firm. Be firm! Don't be defensive, don't be offensive either; you do not have to exchange insults with the troll as that's exactly what he wants from you- don't give it to him. Be the adult in the situation as other viewers might be monitoring the situation to see how well you fare. Be calm, be collected. Think about your reputation you are trying to create and how your reply will look to others. You do not have to get angry. Genuinely respond to comments, show empathy. If the mistakes are from you, admit to them. Apologize if need be. You need to build your credibility; this might just be your little way of doing so. Depending on your temperament, the best response to negative comments sometimes is to completely ignore and move on. Silence is golden. Do not feed these trolls. Nevertheless in all you do, ensure you consider all comments (positive or negative) as valuable feedback. If you must engage negative commentators, do so in a positive fashion.

RATINGS

This is a feature used in YouTube to engage the viewer even more apart from traditional comments. It allows your video to be rated by the viewer. Viewers rate by either giving a thumbs up (if the video is good) or thumbs down (if they don't like the video). The option of allowing viewers rate videos lies entirely on you. It should be noted at this point that videos with high ratings rank higher in YouTube search results than poorly rated ones or those with no ratings at all. You can either check **Yes** to allow ratings or **No** to disallow. It is that simple.

CHAPTER 12 MONETIZATION

Monetization in this regards simply means making money on YouTube. So you have done the hard part producing and uploading the videos on YouTube. You did not still stop there; you went ahead employing all the promotional tactics available to make the channel known and seen by many. Is it not time we talked money? We started this fun but demanding journey for the money right? We don't have to lift out feet off the gas now. We are almost there. We are concerned here with ways through which you can monetize your channel and start making on YouTube. It is all about the revenue generation here.

YOUTUBE PARTNERSHIP

Before we start delve into the different revenue generation methods available in YouTube, it is imperative we discuss the prerequisites for making the money. Being a channel owner alone does not qualify you to earn even a dime on YouTube; if wishes were horses, wouldn't all beggars be riding already? To earn on YouTube, you have to be a YouTube Partner and it is no small feat. YouTube partners have access to multiple streams of revenue from YouTube ranging from adverts, YouTube premium subscription fees, channel memberships, selling merchandise and so on. There are certain criteria that must be met to be a YouTube partner. They include;

- You must have at least a thousand (1,000) subscribers on your YouTube channel.
- Your channel videos must have generated 4,000 Watch Time hours over the last 12 months.
- Compliance with all YouTube's policies and guidelines.

- You must have an AdSense account.

With these criteria met, you are edging even closer to the bank. For your channel to be accepted in the YouTube Partner Program -YPP for shorts, the four requirements must be met.

Nobody wants to know how long it took you to get 1,000 people subscribe to your account. If you can create a YouTube account today and still get 1,000 subscribers today, it is still fine. Your channel will be counted as one that has fulfilled that requirement.

For the 4,000 hours of Watch Time on your videos. This means that your videos on your channel must have been watched by people from across the world for 4,000 hours over the last 12 months in view. You can start the count at any time convenient to you but it must not exceed 12 months. YouTube does the counting anyways when you apply for the YouTube partner program. It is interesting to note that live streams also count towards the total of Watch Time. There is a hitch though; when any video is deleted, the Watch Time is removed from the YouTube channel Watch Time hours. Once you attain the Watch-hours required and is made a partner, even if your channel falls below the minimum 4,000 hours benchmark, YouTube will not automatically kick you out.

To constantly monitor your progress towards attaining the prerequisites for partnership, follow these simple steps

- Click on **your logo** located in the top right corner of the YouTube page.

- Click on the **YouTube Studio Beta**.

All the analytics you need to ascertain your status are all there for you to see. Alternatively, you can decide to;

- Go to Other Features
- Click on **Status and Features**

The prompts bring forth a monetization box. On clicking **Learn More**, your current standing with the subscribers and Watch Time hours will be displayed. After going through the first two processes, next up is where YouTube rigorously checks your channel to ascertain for sure if it is in compliance with its policy and guidelines. One of such YouTube's policies is the copyright policy. If there is any copyrighted content in your channel, chances are high that you will never be accepted. To be on the safer side, before applying to the program, it is advised you critically go through your channel and dispose of the necessary skeletons.

And then finally, to be able to earn money on YouTube, you need to be paid through a channel-AdSense account. If you already have an AdSense account, you just have to link it to YouTube as it can still be used. However, I am assuming you do not have one so you have to set up one during the program application process with these simple steps;

- Go to your YouTube channel
- Go to YouTube Studio, then click on **Settings**, then on **Channel**, and on **Status and Features**
- Click on **Enable**. You should get an **Apply For Monetization page** here
- Click on the **Start** button of Read and agree to the **YouTube Partner Program Terms**
- Click on **I accept**
- Click the start button of the **Sign up for AdSense**
- Choose the Gmail account linked to your channel
- Select your country and also choose your customized help and performance suggestions.
- Read and accept the terms and conditions

- Click on the **Create An Account** button

This should redirect you to the payment address details page where you will enter your complete address and phone number exactly as it is. Do I need to stress on the need it is to enter the details correctly? I hope not. Upon submission of the payment address details, Google reviews the account and sends the approval notification within a week.

MONETIZING YOUR VIDEOS WITH ADS

There are different types of Ad formats on YouTube. Each of them has its own strengths and peculiar tactic of grabbing the viewer's attention. The formats include;

- Display Ads (this is mandatory, but works for desktop version only)
- Overlay Ads (which works for Desktop only)
- Sponsored cards Ads (which works for all devices)
- Skippable Video Ads (which works for all devices)

Ensure to enable all types of Ads in the **Set Monetization Preferences** so as to increase your revenue.

GOOD AD PRACTICES

Here, we are interested in discussing those features that make an advertisement achieve its purpose. We are going to be keeping them short and concise as we have already discussed some of the concepts in the course of this book. For an advert to achieve its purpose and rake in the money we so desire, it should be;

- Kept between 15 and 60 seconds. YouTube Ads should have just two things- message and presentation. The shorter it is the better. Nobody wants to be bored with the lengthy talks.
- It should be captivating.
- The audience should relate to the advert. It should be able to empathize with their needs.

- It should then be associated as the solution to the need.
- It should clearly show your brand in action. Treat every new advertisement as though you are treating a new audience. Clearly show your brand in the advert and what it offers. Do not assume anyone knows already.
- Adverts should be designed for mobile devices too. Research has shown that a great percentage of YouTube views are on mobile devices. Therefore, it is imperative you design ads that are as well compatible with mobile devices. You don't want mobile device users missing out on your message because of the technological hitch.
- Make sure the viewer clearly understands what you want him to do. Utilize the call to action option very well. Appeal to the viewer in clear terms to subscribe to your channel or shop for your products. Either ways, be clear in your presentation what you want the viewer to do.

Don't be ashamed or scared to say it out. No one ever made money being scared or ashamed.

SELLING MERCHANDISE Merchandising is a cool way of making money on YouTube. Almost all the celebrities sell stuff on YouTube. Drake for example, sells t-shirts. If these celebrities who are presumably rich already still sell merchandise on YouTube, how much more, you. The earlier you started putting sentiments aside and pursuing YouTube as pure business, the better. In selling merchandise, your brand is everything. You should not go about selling what does not represent your brand. Your merchandise has to represent your connection with your audience. It is also advised to have a landing page or shop outside YouTube. But then, you should always link it directly to your videos. Moreover, ensure you enable your YouTube partner merchandise shelf feature if you are eligible. Remember that you probably will not sell any of your merchandise if you do not promote them. A great promotion tactic is to wear your merchandise in your video, if they are not wearable articles, use them. Be sure to make it visible in your videos. You may also wish to feature viewers who have bought theirs; it will motivate others to buy. Always remember to thank those who have bought.

CROWDFUNDING You are still keen on making money right? It would not come easy though and you may be in need of money to take care of stuff before it eventually comes. You may be in need of money to get necessary equipment to set up your craft. This money will not fall from the skies. What do you do then? You may have to consider trying crowd funding out any of these days. One way that many YouTube users make money is through crowd funding. It can be intended for a personal project, a community project, or just about any project. It is one of the common ways of soliciting for donations online now. Before embarking on a crowd funding project, your goals should be detailed so that people will know what they are donating to. Nobody would donate money for you to use and take your girlfriend/ boyfriend out on a date or any other similar flimsy reason. An appealing reason should be thought of and sold convincingly to the audience. People need to know what to expect when you finally succeed as well. Ensure to set a target amount you want to meet if not even surpass. Next is setting up an account on a platform to achieve this aim. Patreon is a top choice for recurring funding. It is a crowd funding platform where patrons donate to help artists keep doing their work and get paid on a regular basis while doing so. To set up apatreon account, these detailed steps should serve as a guide;

- Click on **Sign up** on the Patreon homepage and fill the necessary fields
- You may decide to signup directly with Facebook
- Click on **Create on Patreon**. It is the logo in the upper right corner of the page.
- Patreon redirects you to the homepage where you click the **Start my Page**.

In creating your Patreon page, the site guides you through the basics. The Patreon page should be taken seriously as its your face on the platform. Include what you intend to create and what your audience will get in return when they invest in you. It can be in the form of a video. There is also a room for adding profile picture and a cover photo. They should be in the **About** section of your profile. Utilize them well. Do I need to remind you to link your social media accounts? Also choose a username that becomes your Patreon URL. Have content and rewards ready for your donors. Be sure to include your goals in your profile. It is advised to have more than one goal.

LICENSING YOUR CONTENT If a comic skit should go viral on the social media, it wouldn't come as a surprise for CNN or any other leading media outlet to want to get their hands on it so as to replay it for their viewers. The same thing happens in YouTube. When a video goes viral, other media bodies and websites would want to air the content, by so doing they are paying you if the content is licensed. Therefore, ensure you license your most successful works to the media.

To license your content;

- Ensure to keep your updated contact details on your **About** page. This is to make you always reachable in the event that an offer turns up.
- Sign up to a video rights community.

AFFILIATION AND BRAND SPONSORSHIP

Affiliations and brand sponsorships are popular ways for YouTubeusers to make money. Interestingly, you do not even have to give YouTube a cut of the earnings because here, you make deals directly with the brands. They pay you directly likewise and not through YouTube. The problem now lies in getting the right brand that can sponsor you. The surest bet of getting a good brand to sponsor you is when you are able to offer them a large and engaged audience. You can also get them to sponsor you when your content is relevant to their target market. A brand will never sponsor someone who cannot speak their language. However, quality is crucial when you are looking for a brand to sponsor you. Be sure to adhere to Google's Ad policies of bring transparent whilst embarking on the advertising campaign. Your audience should be aware you are advertising to them.

CHANNEL MEMBERSHIP

The YouTube channel membership is a paid program where viewers are allowed to join your channel through monthly payments. They in turn get freebies such as emoji, badges, and other goods.

To be eligible for channel memberships, the following criteria have to be met;

- Your channel must have at least a thousand (1,000) subscribers.
- Your channel should already be in the YouTube Partner Program.
- You must be 18 years and over.
- Your channel should not have a significant number of ineligible videos.
- You must comply with YouTube's terms and policies.
- You must be located in one of the available locations.

Thank you for reading and best of luck.

Richard Boag

www.ingramcontent.com/pod-product-compliance
Ingram Content Group UK Ltd.
Pitfield, Milton Keynes, MK11 3LW, UK
UKHW021911190726
13853UKWH00002B/620